A Pirate, I Be!

R.A. Martinez

Published by R.A. Martinez
Auburn, NY 13021, USA

Written Work Copyright © 2018 by Rick Martinez

Illustrations Copyright © 2018 by Kristine Balog
All rights reserved

A REGISTERED TRADEMARK—

Library of Congress Control Number: 2018912951

ISBN 978-1-7329511-1-2

Printed in the United States of America

All rights reserved. No part of this publication may be reproduced or dispersed in any form or by any means (electronic, photocopying, digital, recording, or otherwise), without prior written permission of the copyright owner and publisher of this book.

Author R.A. Martinez is no stranger amongst the community. He volunteers his time to libraries and schools, reading to the children as a pirate. A Pirate, I Be! is R.A.'s first amongst a long list of children's books to come.

From maps to compasses and sorts.
To keep us going,
from port to ports!

www.ingramcontent.com/pod-product-compliance
Lightning Source LLC
Chambersburg PA
CBHW061146070526
44584CB00033B/4439